Original title:
Beyond the Stars

Copyright © 2024 Creative Arts Management OÜ
All rights reserved.

Author: Adeline Fairfax
ISBN HARDBACK: 978-9916-90-068-0
ISBN PAPERBACK: 978-9916-90-069-7

Starlight Serenade

In the quiet night sky,
Stars whisper and sigh,
Melodies gently flow,
Underneath the moon's glow.

Crickets play their tune,
Dancing 'neath the moon,
A symphony of peace,
Where all worries cease.

Waves of silver light,
Guide us through the night,
Dreams take vibrant flight,
In this tranquil sight.

Hearts aligned in sync,
As we pause and think,
Under the starlit veil,
Love's softest tale.

Oracles from the Dark Matter

Amidst the void and gloom,
Whispers speak of doom,
Galaxies intertwine,
In this grand design.

Echoes of ancient lore,
From realms that we explore,
Cosmic truths unfold,
As mysteries are told.

Stars, the silent guides,
Through infinite tides,
Casting shadows deep,
Awakening from sleep.

Questions of the night,
In the absence of light,
Voices of the past,
In the dark, they cast.

Navigating the Midnight Ocean

Beneath the twilight dome,
We drift far from home,
Oceans vast and wide,
Secrets they confide.

Waves crash, then retreat,
To a rhythmic beat,
The sailors sing loud,
In the night, be proud.

Stars shimmer on the waves,
Guiding us like brave,
Navigators of fate,
To horizons great.

Each gust, a soft sigh,
Reminds us, we fly,
Over depths unknown,
To distant shores grown.

Heartbeats of Distant Worlds

In the stillness we feel,
A pulse that is real,
From worlds far away,
In the cosmos' sway.

Every star a heart,
Playing its own part,
Beating in the night,
With a gentle light.

Whispers from afar,
In the cosmic bar,
Where love transcends time,
In a rhythmic rhyme.

In the dark, we blend,
Our journeys extend,
Together we'll find,
The links that bind.

In the Embrace of the Cosmos

Stars whisper secrets in the deep night,
Galaxies spinning in celestial flight.
Nebulas glow in a vibrant display,
While comets dance in a fleeting ballet.

Planets hum softly, a rhythmic tune,
Beneath the watchful gaze of the moon.
Time stretches thin in this cosmic sea,
Where dreams awaken and minds roam free.

Twilight's Cosmic Embrace

As daylight fades, a blanket unfolds,
Twilight's soft hues, a story retold.
The sky transforms, a canvas of dreams,
Where starlight whispers and the night gleams.

Crickets play symphonies in the breeze,
Echoes of stardust drift through the trees.
Each twinkle a promise, a wish in disguise,
In twilight's embrace, the universe lies.

Spheres of Light

In the depths of space, orbs gently sway,
Floating like thoughts that wander and play.
Radiant spheres in a cosmic ballet,
Illuminating paths where shadows betray.

Each flicker of light tells a tale untold,
Of journeys uncharted, of destinies bold.
They guide our souls through the velvet night,
In the vastness of space, we find our light.

Uncharted Constellations

Beyond the known, where the wild stars gleam,
New constellations weave a mystic dream.
With every glance, the stories unfold,
In the canvas of night, their secrets behold.

Adventures await in the stellar expanse,
Where planets and comets in beauty dance.
Lost to the world, we journey so far,
In uncharted realms guided by a star.

Starlit Journeys

Under a quilt of night,
Dreams take their flight,
Whispers of the stars,
Guide us from afar.

Through the cosmic mist,
Lost in the twist,
Where shadows dissolve,
And mysteries evolve.

With every twinkling light,
We chase our delight,
Searching for a sign,
To know that you're mine.

In this vast expanse,
We find our chance,
To dance among the skies,
And let our spirits rise.

Navigating the Milky Way

In the river of stars,
We sail through the dark,
Each twinkle a map,
Guiding our spark.

Galaxies swirl around,
As we chart our course,
With hope in our hearts,
And unstoppable force.

Through nebulae bright,
We find our true way,
With laughter and light,
In the Milky Way.

A journey divine,
In this cosmic ballet,
Together we'll wander,
And never dismay.

Secrets of the Celestial Sea

Beneath the moon's gaze,
The cosmos reveals,
Hidden tales untold,
In the starlight it heals.

Waves of constellations,
Crash upon the night,
Whispers of long lost
In the ethereal light.

With each gentle breeze,
Secrets drift high,
From the depths of the sea,
To the vast open sky.

In silence we listen,
To the universe's song,
Unlocking the mysteries,
Where our hearts belong.

Comets and Wishes

As comets streak by,
We make our desires,
Catching dreams in flight,
Like sparks from the fires.

With a flicker of hope,
And a heart all aglow,
We reach for the stars,
As they dance and flow.

Every wish held tight,
In the night's embrace,
Guided by starlight,
In this timeless place.

We blaze through the sky,
Together we'll fly,
On comets of dreams,
With wishes that rise.

Secrets of the Celestial Canvas

Stars twinkle softly, dreams unfold,
Brush strokes of starlight, tales untold.
Galaxies whisper in night's embrace,
Shadows dance gently in cosmic space.

Nebulas cradle secrets in hues,
Colors blend softly, rich and true.
Each stroke a story of time and fate,
Crafting a wonder, a timeless state.

Songs of the Celestial Wanderers

Voices of comets in the night air,
Chasing the echoes, a magical flare.
Planets hum gently, a lullaby tune,
Celestial wanderers, beneath the moon.

Moons sway like dancers, silver and bright,
Tales of the cosmos, a wondrous sight.
Each note a journey through infinite space,
A symphony woven, time's gentle grace.

Threads of the Universe's Fabric

Spun from starlight, threads intertwine,
Connecting the cosmos, both yours and mine.
Woven through eons, patterns they weave,
Stories of worlds that we deeply believe.

In the loom of existence, each fiber gleams,
Binding the heavens to our earthly dreams.
Colors of life in filament bright,
A tapestry glowing with cosmic light.

Through the Veil of Cosmic Wonders

Parting the curtains of night's gentle shroud,
Revealing the wonders, both silent and loud.
Galactic horizons where mysteries lie,
Searching for answers beneath the vast sky.

Visions of stardust, a glimpse of the past,
Through the veil's whispers, we wander fast.
Each planet a story, each star a guide,
Through cosmic dimensions, we boldly glide.

Lanterns in the Galactic Sea

In the dark where stardust swirls,
Bright lanterns twinkle, like precious pearls.
They guide the ships of dreams uncharted,
Their glow ignites the souls, once parted.

Waves of silence in the cosmic grey,
Each flicker whispers, 'Come, let's play.'
Beneath the veil of the night so vast,
We sail through shadows, future and past.

Nebulae unfold like tales untold,
Their vibrant colors, a sight to behold.
With every glimmer, hearts entwine,
In the galactic dance, we feel divine.

So, cast your nets into this sea,
Gather the lanterns, set your spirit free.
In the depths where the quiet sings,
Hope floats gently on celestial wings.

Chasing the Fragments of Light

Fragments of light in the endless dark,
Chasing them down, hoping to spark.
Each shimmer whispers a story's thread,
Of worlds forgotten and paths once tread.

We run through the cosmos, starry and bright,
With every heartbeat, we seek the light.
In the vastness where shadows blend,
We reach for the glow, our hearts to mend.

In the tapestry where night meets day,
Fragments glisten, leading the way.
Through the silence, our dreams entwine,
As we chase the ghost of the divine.

With every glow, our souls ignite,
Chasing the fragments, we embrace the night.
For in the darkness, we find our way,
With pieces of light that never sway.

Where the Universe Begins

Where the universe begins, a spark ignites,
Unfolding galaxies and cosmic sights.
From nothingness blooms the boundless sky,
In this cradle of stars, we learn to fly.

The whispers of comets, a celestial song,
In the heart of chaos, we find where we belong.
Dreams intertwined with cosmic threads,
In the tapestry of time, our curiosity spreads.

Each heartbeat echoes through the void's embrace,
A dance of creation, a slow, timeless grace.
Where the universe breathes with endless might,
We stand in awe of its brilliant light.

In this sacred space of endless night,
We search for answers, a guiding light.
Where the universe begins, we take our stand,
As voyagers sailing through the stars' command.

Tales from the Edge of the Void

From the edge of the void, stories arise,
Whispers of wonders, written in the skies.
Galaxies swirl, their secrets unfold,
In the silence of night, their tales are told.

Echoes of time drift on starlit streams,
Illuminating our darkest dreams.
Here at the brink, where shadows collide,
We ponder the stars, and what they hide.

Each black hole cradles a mystery deep,
Guarding the knowledge that stars long keep.
In the abyss where silence reigns,
We gather the lore of celestial pains.

The edge of the void holds secrets vast,
Of journeys taken and moments passed.
With every tale, our hearts align,
At the cusp of forever, our souls intertwine.

The Starlit Path to Wonder

In the stillness of the night,
Stars flicker like a wish,
Guiding hearts towards the light,
In dreams, we find our bliss.

Each twinkle tells a tale,
Of journeys yet to take,
From the moonlit, silver trail,
To realms where silence wakes.

Whispers of the ancient skies,
Fill the air with gentle grace,
As we walk where magic lies,
In this vast, enchanting space.

Step by step, we weave our fate,
With each starlit breath we crave,
Together through this wondrous gate,
Where every moment we are brave.

Rising with the Cosmic Dawn

Awake to the blush of morn,
As shadows softly flee,
The universe is reborn,
In vibrant hues, we see.

Petals of the sun unfold,
Wrapping earth in warm embrace,
Golden stories yet untold,
Igniting our human grace.

With each step, new dreams ignite,
And hope begins to rise,
Emerging from the night,
As stars yield to the skies.

Let us dance in twilight's glow,
To the rhythm of the sphere,
In this cosmic ebb and flow,
Together, we persevere.

Whispers from the Aurora

Vibrant hues dance in the night,
Softly they weave, a shimmering sight.
Whispers of magic, secrets untold,
In crimson and emerald, their stories unfold.

Beneath the vast canvas, dreams take flight,
Guided by stars, we bask in their light.
Nature's own symphony, a celestial song,
In whispers so gentle, where we all belong.

Chasing Shooting Stars

Across the sky they race and twirl,
Brief fleeting glimpses that make hearts whirl.
In the silence of night, hopes take form,
Chasing the wishes where wonders swarm.

Each streak a promise, a silent plea,
Carried by wishes, a shared reverie.
We reach for the heavens, hands stretched wide,
As dreams ignite boldly, on stardust we glide.

The Language of Light

Colors that speak without a sound,
In every shadow, a truth is found.
Morning whispers, a soft embrace,
The sun's golden laughter lights up the space.

Moonbeams shimmer like secrets shared,
In twilight's glow, we're unprepared.
Light weaves stories, both near and far,
A radiant language, our guiding star.

Galactic Heartbeats

In the depths of the cosmos, echoes resound,
Galaxies swirling in a dance profound.
Every heartbeat echoes, a cosmic sign,
Connected by stardust, your soul and mine.

Time flows like rivers, bringing us near,
In the silence of space, we lose all fear.
With every pulse, our spirits ignite,
As we dance through the darkness, embracing the light.

The Hidden Symphony of the Cosmos

In the depths where stars are born,
Whispers of light break the dawn.
Each twinkle tells a tale untold,
Of dreams and destinies, bright and bold.

Galaxies dance in silent grace,
A cosmic waltz, a timeless embrace.
Harmony sings in the dark expanse,
Our hearts tune in to this vast romance.

Nebulas swirl in vibrant hues,
Painting the skies with celestial clues.
With each heartbeat, the universe sways,
In the rhythm of life, it forever plays.

Unraveling the Night's Secrets

The moon hangs low, a silver thread,
Casting dreams where shadows tread.
Stars are secrets, waiting to be found,
In the silence of night, whispers abound.

Beneath the canopy, stories unfold,
Ancient mysteries quietly told.
The cool breeze carries a sigh,
As time slips softly, drifting by.

Glowing embers of thoughts ignite,
In the solitude of the night's delight.
We unravel the threads of fate,
In the embrace of the cosmos, we wait.

Tides of Cosmic Awareness

Waves of starlight wash ashore,
Each pulse a call, forevermore.
The ocean of time flows like a dream,
In cosmic currents, we drift and gleam.

With every tide, our minds expand,
Grasping the wonders that life has planned.
Awareness blooms in the dark blue swell,
In the depths of knowledge, we choose to dwell.

Celestial bodies in perfect sway,
Guide our thoughts along the way.
In unity, we rise and fall,
Listening closely to the universe's call.

Fragments of Existence in the Void

Scattered stardust in endless night,
Each fragment glimmers with quiet light.
In the void, we see reflections clear,
Of love and longing, hope and fear.

Amidst the silence, we find our place,
In the tapestry of time, we trace.
Every moment, a thread we weave,
In the dark, together we believe.

Echoes of being, softly they hum,
In the vast unknown, we're never numb.
Embracing the void, we learn to soar,
In the fragments of existence, we explore.

Galaxies Unfold

Stars shimmer in the night,
Spinning tales of ancient light.
Nebulas cradle dreams anew,
In the vastness, hope breaks through.

Across the void, whispers sigh,
Time reflects like a painted sky.
In the silence, pulses race,
Carving paths in cosmic space.

Planets dance in quiet grace,
Orbiting an uncharted place.
Eons pass, yet still they twirl,
In this endless, starlit whirl.

Galaxies unfold their arms,
Embracing all of nature's charms.
In the dark, a spark ignites,
Guiding us through endless nights.

The Dance of Distant Suns

A veil of dusk adorns the sky,
While distant suns begin to fly.
They twinkle with alluring light,
Painting dreams that pierce the night.

Each solar burst, a radiant call,
Echoing through the cosmic hall.
For every flash, a story spun,
In the dance of distant suns.

Comets trail with fiery tails,
Whispering secrets of the gales.
They weave through constellations bright,
Bathing the void in pure delight.

As shadows stretch and fade away,
The universe begins to play.
In cosmic waltz, we find our way,
Eclipsing the night, welcoming day.

Dreams Among the Nebulae

In the cradle of colorful fog,
Where stardust swirls, and wonders log.
Faint echoes of dreams start to bloom,
Luminous whispers light the gloom.

Nebulae hold secrets tight,
Cradling visions in soft twilight.
In swirling hues, tales reside,
Where worlds collide and hopes abide.

Particles dance, entwined in grace,
Creating a vibrant cosmic space.
The heart of night, a canvas wide,
Where our deepest dreams will glide.

Among the stars, in timeless flight,
We chase our hopes into the night.
As nebulae flicker and sway,
We find our paths and drift away.

Astral Horizons

Up above the world so high,
Are horizons where dreams lie.
Streaks of light embrace the dawn,
Whispers of the stars are drawn.

Infinity spreads out its arms,
Offering peace amidst the charms.
In every gleam, a story we find,
A journey of the heart and mind.

Locked in time, we weave our fate,
On astral paths, we navigate.
With cosmic winds beneath our wings,
We soar where starlight ever sings.

As horizons shift and fade from view,
The vast expanse invites us through.
In the embrace of endless skies,
We chase the dawn, where silence lies.

Into the Embrace of the Unknown

Whispers call from shadows deep,
Secrets hidden, dreams to keep.
Paths uncharted, visions bright,
Into the night, we take our flight.

Winds of change, a swirling tide,
Hearts aflame, we won't abide.
Fearless steps into the dark,
With every spark, we leave our mark.

Eager souls, with hopes to find,
Answers waiting, intertwined.
In the depths, we dare to dive,
In the unknown, we feel alive.

Stars above, they guide our way,
Sparking courage for the fray.
Into the embrace, we shall go,
Trusting in what we do not know.

Luminaries of a Forgotten Cosmos

Once they shone, a grand array,
Now mere echoes of yesterday.
In the void, their stories sleep,
Wonders forgotten, secrets deep.

Galaxies swirl in silent grace,
Faint reminders of a lost place.
With every twinkle, tales unfold,
Of heroes brave and lovers bold.

Ancient dreams in starlit dust,
Whispers of hope, a cosmic trust.
We reach out to touch the light,
In the distance, memories ignite.

Now we wander through the night,
Seeking glimmers of old delight.
Luminaries in our hearts endure,
Guiding us home, steadfast and pure.

Emissaries of the Night Sky

Stars like messengers above,
Carrying tales of peace and love.
In their glow, we find our guide,
Through the realms where dreams abide.

Celestial bodies, dance they do,
Painting stories in shades of blue.
Every spark a voice so clear,
Calling us closer, drawing near.

Emissaries of distant lands,
With gentle light, they take our hands.
In their presence, fears dissolve,
In the mystery, we evolve.

As the night unfolds its shroud,
We gather strength, we feel so proud.
In the sky, our hopes align,
Emissaries of the divine.

The Silence Between the Stars

In the quiet, moments pause,
Time suspends without a cause.
Within the void, we find our peace,
Nature's breath, a soothing release.

Stars ignite the velvet dark,
Each a wish, a whispered spark.
Yet in silence, truths emerge,
In the stillness, hearts converge.

Every heartbeat resonates,
Across the cosmos' wide expanse.
A connection felt, unspoken thread,
In this silence, all is said.

Beneath the heavens, vast and wide,
We find a place where dreams abide.
Here in the calm, we are free,
The silence, our eternity.

Tethered to the Celestial Drift

In the whispers of the night sky,
Stars weave tales of ancient lore.
Galaxies spin in silent sighs,
Each twinkle opens a door.

Floating on the cosmic breeze,
Hearts anchored to dreams untold.
The universe sways with ease,
Embracing warmth against the cold.

Planets dance in a grand ballet,
Chasing shadows, crafting light.
We drift along this astral way,
In celestial embrace, take flight.

Time unfolds like a paper map,
Constellations guide our path.
With every star, we close the gap,
In the cosmos, find our wrath.

Horizons of a New Tomorrow

The dawn breaks with gentle grace,
A canvas painted in hues of gold.
Whispers of hope begin to trace,
Stories waiting to be told.

Fields awaken beneath the sun,
Each flower unfolds its dream.
Together hearts beat as one,
In every sparkle, a shared gleam.

Mountains stand tall, proud and high,
Guardians of our fleeting time.
We reach for the depths of the sky,
In unity, our spirits climb.

With every step, a chance to grow,
To chase the shadows of the past.
Horizons shape what we'd like to know,
Together, our dreams will last.

The Starlit Map to Dreams

Beneath the vast, expansive night,
We chart our course among the stars.
Constellations flicker with light,
Guiding us past fate's bizarre.

Each dream a pin on this bright sheet,
A journey sewn with hopes and fears.
In whispers soft, our hearts repeat,
The stories born of countless years.

Through silvery skies, we dare to soar,
Finding solace in the space.
With gravity's pull, we seek for more,
In starlit patterns, we find grace.

Maps drawn in glimmers softly glow,
Reminding us where we belong.
The universe holds treasures to show,
In every pulse, a vibrant song.

Musings of a Starlit Mind

Thoughts dance like fireflies at dusk,
Whirling in the cosmic tide.
In every shadow, a hidden husk,
A journey where dreams coincide.

Silent echoes of midnight calls,
As galaxies whisper their creed.
In the stillness, a wonder stalls,
A quest that only hearts can lead.

Through tangled thoughts and stardust dreams,
Ideas flicker and glow like sparks.
In the chaos, a sense redeems,
Illuminating all of our arcs.

Let us wander, let us roam,
In a starlit mind, we find peace.
Among celestial thoughts, we comb,
In this realm, our spirits seize.

The Orbit of Hope

In the darkness, stars ignite,
Whispers of dreams take flight.
Circling shadows, soft and bright,
A dance of fate in the night.

Hope like a comet, swift and bold,
Tales of courage yet untold.
Guiding spirits, hearts unfold,
In the warmth of promises gold.

Through the trials, light will bend,
Towards horizons that transcend.
Every heartbeat, a faithful friend,
In the orbit, we ascend.

Together we rise, a cosmic seam,
Tethered tight to every dream.
In the silence, we all scream,
Finding peace in the cosmic beam.

Lunar Reveries

Silver whispers through the trees,
A gentle touch upon the seas.
In soft glow, the moment frees,
Dancing worlds in lunar breeze.

Dreamscapes woven, threads of light,
Floating softly, day and night.
In the stillness, stars ignite,
Reflections born of pure delight.

Moonbeams cast their magic glow,
Painting paths where passions flow.
In the silence, wisdom grows,
As the heart with wonder knows.

With each phase, the mind expands,
Lost in time's eternal hands.
In lunar dreams, the spirit stands,
Connected deep as night commands.

Celestial Abode

In the heavens, wonders dwell,
Echoes of a timeless spell.
Amongst the stars, we weave and swell,
In this place, all dreams compel.

Galaxies spin in radiant dance,
Every glance a universe's chance.
In this realm, we seek romance,
With cosmic love, our souls entrance.

Shooting stars, like wishes fly,
Beneath the vast and endless sky.
In this abode, we cannot lie,
For in the light, our hopes comply.

Every heartbeat, a star's embrace,
We find our rhythm, pulse and chase.
In the cosmos, we carve our space,
In celestial harmony, our grace.

The Edge of Infinity

Where horizons kiss the sky,
Time and space gently sigh.
In the silence, we ask why,
As stars in unison reply.

A leap beyond what eyes can see,
In the depths, we find the key.
To unlock realms of mystery,
Embracing vast eternity.

On the edge, we hear the call,
A timeless echo, spheric ball.
Each heartbeat, a rise and fall,
In this dance, we lose it all.

In the void, we find our truth,
In the journey, the light of youth.
On the edge, we share our proof,
As infinity cradles our ruth.

The Luminary's Reverie

In whispers soft, the starlight sings,
A tapestry of dreams it brings.
Each twinkle holds a secret past,
A fleeting glance, too sweet to last.

We dance beneath the silver hues,
In twilight's grace, we share our views.
The cosmos deep, a beckoning call,
A boundless joy, an endless thrall.

As moonbeams weave through night's embrace,
We find our truth, our sacred space.
The luminary guides our flight,
To realms unseen, to purest light.

Together lost, yet found in dreams,
We float on hope, like gentle streams.
In reverie, the stars inspire,
Our souls ablaze, like cosmic fire.

Chasing Echoes in the Astral Glow

In shadows deep, we hear the sound,
Of whispers soft, where dreams abound.
Chasing echoes, hand in hand,
Through fields of light, a mystic land.

The constellations twirl and play,
As time suspends, we drift away.
In every pulse, the universe speaks,
A vibrant dance, where time still seeks.

We chase the light, the stardust trails,
With every heart, the journey sails.
In astral glow, our spirits soar,
Through timeless realms, forevermore.

Each echo shapes the infinite night,
A symphony of pure delight.
In cosmic dreams, we find our song,
A love that glows, forever strong.

Celestial Sojourns

As comets blaze through velvet skies,
We wander far, where starlight lies.
In cosmic winds, our tales unfold,
Of journeys vast, and dreams retold.

Planets spin in graceful arcs,
While lunar beams ignite the sparks.
We sail on dreams, on tides of love,
A dance that echoes, stars above.

Through galaxies, we roam and glide,
With constellations as our guide.
In every pulse, the beauty reigns,
A harmony that soothes our pains.

In sojourns bold, we find our peace,
A realm where worries cease to cease.
With every star, our spirits play,
In cosmic grace, we drift away.

The Art of Cosmic Infinity

In strokes of light, the heavens paint,
A masterpiece, both bold and faint.
With every star, a story blooms,
In cosmic halls, where silence looms.

The galaxies weave a grand design,
A rhythm pure, a force divine.
In every swirl, the truth unfolds,
The art of time, as life beholds.

We journey through, where wonders blend,
With every curve, our spirits mend.
In cosmic depth, we find our way,
An endless dance, by night and day.

Embracing all, the vast unknown,
In unity, we're never alone.
The art of cosmic infinity,
Awakens hearts, sets spirits free.

Illuminated by Otherworldly Flames

In the heart of the night sky,
A flicker dances bright and bold,
Colors swirl with cosmic grace,
Melodies of the stars unfold.

Veils of light weave tales untold,
Whispers brush against the soul,
Each spark a wish, a dream of old,
Where the universe feels whole.

Beneath the cosmic tapestry,
I wander through the endless space,
In every gleam, a mystery,
A touch of time, a warm embrace.

We're illuminated by their flames,
Chasing visions lost in night,
In the dance of cosmic games,
We find ourselves in shadowed light.

A Journey to the Twinkling Expanse

Upon the wings of a comet's tail,
I soar through skies of midnight hue,
Each star a compass, a holy grail,
Guiding my heart to realms anew.

Nebulas cradle dreams in bloom,
Galaxies whisper of ancient lore,
In the quiet vastness, I feel the room,
Of cosmic wonders waiting to explore.

Fragments of light in endless flight,
Carving paths through the cosmic sea,
Every twinkle a beacon of light,
Calling me home, where I long to be.

As I journey through the night's embrace,
I shed my fears, I shed my doubt,
In the embrace of this celestial space,
I discover what life is all about.

Dreams Woven in Stardust

In silence where the cosmos breathes,
Dreams are spun from glittering threads,
A tapestry where starlight weaves,
Hopes and wishes gently spreads.

With every twinkle, stories rise,
Of worlds unseen and lives unknown,
In the fabric of the night skies,
I plant my heart, my dreams, my own.

Through the veil of the night, I roam,
Chasing visions on the celestial stream,
In the cradle of the endless dome,
I lose myself in every dream.

Woven in stardust, we all belong,
In the cosmos' embrace, we unite,
Guided by a chorus of ancient songs,
We find our way through the endless night.

The Call of the Distant Suns

Far beyond where shadows play,
Distant suns begin to hum,
Their whispers travel night and day,
A serenade from where they're from.

With every pulse, a promise made,
To wander hearts like drifting leaves,
In the tapestry of time displayed,
A universe that gently weaves.

I heed the call of their radiant glow,
A beacon in the darkened sea,
Each spark a thread, a place to go,
Where dreams and destinies intertwine free.

Oh, how the distant stars inspire,
Filling my spirit with cosmic light,
Guiding me deeper into desire,
As I chase the suns of the night.

Voices from the Luminous Depths

Whispers drift from ocean's core,
Echoes of the ages soar.
Deep beneath the waves they sing,
Tales of loss and hope they bring.

A melody of ancient light,
Guiding souls through darkest night.
In currents strong, their stories flow,
In depths where only dreamers go.

The moon casts shadows on the sea,
A symphony of mystery.
Each voice a spark, a light anew,
A dance of spirits, bold and true.

In silence, they find their release,
A harmony that brings us peace.
From luminous depths, they arise,
Filling the world with their cries.

In the Arms of the Universe

Cradled by the starry night,
Galaxies whisper, soft and bright.
In cosmic arms, we sway and spin,
A journey starts where dreams begin.

The stardust wraps us, warm and near,
With every heartbeat, we draw near.
Planets dance in a graceful ballet,
Guiding us through the vast array.

Time unfolds like a gentle sigh,
Moments linger, the stardust fly.
Together we drift, lost in bliss,
In the universe's sweet abyss.

With every breath, the cosmos gleams,
In the arms of night, we weave our dreams.
The infinite sky, vast and bold,
Whispers secrets yet untold.

Sandcastles on the Milky Way

Grains of stardust fall like sand,
Each galaxy crafted by gentle hand.
With laughter we build, high and grand,
Castles bright in a cosmic land.

The tides of time wash dreams away,
Yet whispered wishes still hold sway.
In the stillness, our spirits play,
Creating worlds where we can stay.

As comets trail their fiery light,
We dance in shadows of the night.
Each castle glimmers, fragile, bright,
A testament to love's delight.

Built from hope and timeless grace,
In the Milky Way, we've found our place.
Though storms may come to sweep away,
Together, we'll build anew each day.

The Dance of Celestial Spirits

In twilight glows, the spirits waltz,
Between the stars, no fear, no faults.
They twirl with grace around the moon,
A dance eternal, a sacred tune.

With every glow, a story spun,
Uniting worlds, the many, one.
They weave their light in cosmic threads,
In harmony, where silence spreads.

The constellations hum along,
A symphony, a timeless song.
Each step a whisper, each spin a chance,
In the night's embrace, the spirits dance.

And when we gaze at skies above,
We feel their pulse, their endless love.
In the heart of night, they create art,
In the dance of stars, we find our heart.

Beyond the Veil of Night

In shadows thick, the whispers glide,
The moonlight dances, a silver tide.
Mysteries swirl in the cool night air,
As dreams awaken, beyond despair.

The stars are lanterns, aglow with grace,
Guardians of secrets in this vast space.
Echoes of stories, the past ignites,
A tapestry woven in crystalline lights.

Fade into silence, the world drifts away,
The heart beats softly, in quiet sway.
Each breath a promise, each sigh a song,
Beyond the veil, where we all belong.

Let go the worries that pull you down,
In night's embrace, wear your crown.
Together we wander, two souls, one light,
Lost in the beauty beyond the night.

Sentinels of the Starry Abyss

Under the dome of a velvet sky,
Sentinels watch as the night slips by.
Stars like diamonds in a sea of black,
Guardians of wishes on celestial track.

With gentle eyes they gleam and glow,
Guiding the dreamers as they flow.
Whispers of cosmos in every breath,
Eternal echoes of life and death.

Their vigil holds stories of all who roam,
Through griefs and joys, they call us home.
Wrapped in tranquility, we find our place,
In the arms of the night, in cosmic embrace.

Beneath their watch, we craft our fate,
With stars as guides, we navigate.
Together, we dance in the starlit mist,
The universe calls, and we can't resist.

The Cosmic Quilt of Dreams

Threads of starlight in the fabric of time,
Sewn with the hopes of a world sublime.
Each patch a story, each stitch a heart,
In the cosmic quilt, we find our part.

Woven with laughter, with love and strife,
Patterns of seasons, the dance of life.
Colors of dusk and the gold of dawn,
In every moment, a chance reborn.

As night settles softly, we dream anew,
Chasing the whispers of skies so blue.
With every breath, we weave our fate,
In the tapestry vast, we cultivate.

Let visions guide you through twilight's veil,
In the cosmic quilt of dreams, we sail.
Together we wander, together we gleam,
In the woven wonders of every dream.

In Search of the Luminous Horizon

Through valleys deep where shadows play,
We journey forth, come what may.
With hearts alight and spirits clear,
In search of horizons, ever near.

The sun will rise to beckon our quest,
A promise written, a welcome guest.
As dawn breaks free from night's embrace,
We chase the light, the endless space.

Beneath the sky, we seek and find,
The luminous trails that guide the blind.
Each step a whisper, each glance a spark,
In the glow of hope, we leave the dark.

Together we wander, hand in hand,
Across the sands of time, we stand.
In search of the horizon, we blaze a way,
Towards the light of a brand new day.

Messages from the Void

In silence deep, the cosmos speaks,
Whispers of stars, their ancient peaks.
Echoes of time, a haunting call,
Secrets hidden, above us all.

Through darkened realms, the shadows glide,
Carrying tales of worlds untried.
Each pulse of light, a story spun,
A dance of dreams, so far, so fun.

Fleeting moments, a cosmic chat,
In every twinkle, a space-time spat.
Messages drift, like dust in air,
Reaching out, beyond despair.

So look above, let your heart roam,
Find in the sky, a celestial home.
For every void, though vast and still,
Holds a spark of life, a dream to fulfill.

The Lullaby of Planets

Softly hums the distant spheres,
Cradling dreams through time and years.
Moonlight dances on silver streams,
While stars weave in and out of dreams.

Gentle whispers of twilight's grace,
As comets glide in endless chase.
Each heartbeat echoes the cosmic rhyme,
A lullaby sung, transcending time.

Planets spin in perfect harmony,
Chasing shadows, finding glee.
In the vastness, stillness swells,
The lullaby of starlit bells.

Rest your soul, let worries fade,
In the symphony of night, be swayed.
For in this peace, the cosmos waits,
To share with you its wondrous fates.

A Voyage Through Starlit Veils

We sail on dreams through velvet night,
Guided by stars, our hearts alight.
Each glimmer leads to realms unknown,
In spaces vast, we find our own.

Nebulae bloom in colors bright,
Painting visions of cosmic flight.
With every breath, the universe calls,
Inviting us to break down walls.

Galaxies swirl in a tender whirl,
As distant suns begin to twirl.
Through starlit veils, our spirits soar,
A voyage glimpsed, forevermore.

So step aboard this craft of dreams,
Let go of fear and silent screams.
In this expanse, we're never alone,
Together, we'll find our way back home.

Fragments of a Distant Realm

Echoes of light from ages passed,
Reveal the secrets of shadows cast.
Fragmented worlds, in stillness found,
Whispers of life in silence abound.

In every shard, a story sleeps,
Of cosmic winds and timeless leaps.
Through the haze of a glowing sight,
We grasp at dreams, embracing light.

Fleeting glimpses of realms remiss,
Where time converges in a cosmic kiss.
Each fragment holds a universe wide,
Inviting wanderers to reside.

So gather 'round the distant glow,
As stardust dances to and fro.
In these fragments, truth awaits,
A distant realm, with open gates.

Letters Written in Meteor Dust

Underneath the starry sky,
Whispers float on cosmic winds.
Ink from comets trails behind,
Messages from distant friends.

Etched in silence, secrets glow,
Each word a spark from worlds unknown.
Fleeting moments caught in flight,
Written softly, dreams have grown.

Windswept echoes tell our tales,
Across the vast and dark expanse.
In these glimmers, hope prevails,
A chance for love, a fated chance.

So we gather the stardust light,
Binding letters with heart and soul.
In the universe's grand design,
We'll find our peace, we'll find our whole.

The Hidden Portals of Night

In the shadows, secrets sigh,
Veiled within the velvet sky.
Portals whisper, beckon near,
Dancing stars, a world of cheer.

Through the darkness, paths unfold,
Mysteries wrapped in silver cold.
Glimmers of a thousand dreams,
Echo softly, or so it seems.

Above, the moonlight spills like wine,
Crafting wonders, pure and fine.
With each breath, we dive and soar,
Into realms unseen before.

Hidden passage, night's embrace,
Time stands still in this sacred space.
As we wander, hearts alight,
We'll unlock the portals of night.

Odyssey Through the Cosmic Sea

Vast horizons, stars ignite,
Our journey starts in endless night.
Galaxies spin, a dance so grand,
Together we traverse this land.

Sailing ships of dreams and fate,
On the waves of time we wait.
Beyond the planets, we will soar,
Discovering treasures, evermore.

With each wave, the cosmos calls,
Whispers of adventure in its thralls.
Mirrored skies, reflections bright,
We navigate through stars' delight.

Beyond the reach of human sight,
Our hearts entwined in cosmic flight.
An odyssey, forever free,
Together through the cosmic sea.

Portraits of Time Beyond Light

Brushstrokes of memory unfold,
Canvas painted in hues of gold.
Moments captured, whispers trace,
Eternal echoes, time's embrace.

Fleeting seconds, shadows cast,
Artistry of stories past.
Framing life in every glance,
In the gallery, we take our chance.

Beyond the veil, where sirens sing,
The past and future intertwine,
Portraits bloom, like flowers bright,
In the realm beyond the light.

Each brushstroke holds a heartbeat's flame,
Tales of joy, and echoes of pain.
In this tapestry we weave,
Time remains; we shall believe.

Boundless Horizons of the Celestial Realm

Across the sky, the stars will gleam,
Infinite worlds, a cosmic dream.
Beyond the veil of night they wait,
Whispers of fate, a silent gate.

Nebulas swirl in hues untold,
Stories of life in stardust gold.
Planets dance in ethereal light,
A symphony of day and night.

Endless vista, horizons wide,
In this realm, our hopes abide.
Each shimmering point, a tale to tell,
In this boundless space, all is well.

Journey through time, we take the flight,
Into the arms of celestial night.
With each breath, we embrace the fate,
Of stars that shine, of dreams that wait.

The Music of the Spheres

In silence deep, the cosmos sings,
A melody of unseen things.
Planets whirl in cosmic dance,
To echo life's eternal chance.

Notes weave through the fabric of space,
A harmony time cannot erase.
Each star a note, in rhythm's flow,
Together they create a glow.

Galaxies spin with a cosmic tune,
Playing softly beneath the moon.
Their whispers drift on cosmic waves,
As long as time, the music saves.

Listen close to the sounds of light,
In the dark, they illuminate the night.
A symphony of worlds intertwined,
In this vastness, freedom we find.

Guardians of the Cosmic Tides

Celestial sentinels in the dark,
Guard the pathways, each bright spark.
With watchful eyes, they weave the fate,
Of worlds unseen, beyond the gate.

In solemn peace, they hold the line,
Steering stars on paths divine.
Through storm and calm, they never waver,
In the vastness, they are the savior.

Eons pass, yet they remain,
Shielding dreams in cosmic rain.
A force unseen, a guiding hand,
In the fabric of space, they stand.

Guardians of tides that ebb and flow,
With gentle might, their energies glow.
To them we look, our hopes abide,
In the heart of the great cosmic tide.

Galaxies Beyond Imagination

Wonders await in black expanses,
Galaxies whirling in cosmic dances.
Colors burst, a radiant show,
In the vastness where dreams can grow.

Each swirl a story, each point a spark,
In the cosmos bright, endless and dark.
We reach with our hearts, to the great unknown,
In every corner, knowledge is sown.

Unseen worlds call to us so clear,
In whispers of light, we hold them dear.
Imagination soars on wings of night,
Chasing horizons, a beckoning light.

From dust to stars, the journey's vast,
In galaxies beyond, the shadows cast.
With open minds, let us explore,
The infinite realms we can't ignore.

Navigators of the Cosmic Mystery

In silence we drift through the vast unknown,
Star maps in hand, with courage we've grown.
Each twinkling light holds a secret untold,
In the fabric of space, a story unfolds.

Guided by whispers of ancient starlight,
We sail through the cosmos, embracing the night.
Galaxies beckon with wonders so bright,
As navigators dream and take flight.

Through black holes and comets, we forge our tale,
On ships made of hope, we dare to set sail.
With charts drawn by stardust, we chase the thrill,
In the cosmic expanse, our hearts beat still.

Together we wander, the curious few,
Exploring the realms where the dreamers break through.
In the mystery's hug, we find our own grace,
Navigators of dreams in this infinite space.

Silhouettes Against the Night Sky

Silhouettes dance on the velvet so deep,
Casting shadows where secrets sleep.
Under the moon, we whisper and sigh,
Figures entwined, against the night sky.

With stars as our witness, we embrace the dark,
In the stillness of night, we spark a new arc.
Each breath a promise, each heartbeat a chance,
As silhouettes waltz in a timeless romance.

The world holds its breath, as dreamers will soar,
Tracing the outlines of worlds we explore.
In the glow of the cosmos, we find our reply,
Bound together forever, against the night sky.

In silence and shadows, our spirits ignite,
A tapestry woven with threads of starlight.
With hope as our compass, we dare to fly,
As silhouettes drift in the breath of the sky.

The Poetry of Interstellar Paths

Beneath the gaze of a million bright eyes,
We write our own verses, as worlds softly rise.
In the poetry of orbits, we dance and we weave,
Interstellar paths where the heart learns to believe.

With each passing comet, a tale is spun,
A symphony of stardust, a race never done.
Through nebulas swirling, our dreams take their form,
In the cradle of cosmos, we weather the storm.

Galactic seas whisper our names in the dark,
On tidal waves of light, we each leave our mark.
In the silence of space, the verses align,
As we scribble the fate of a life so divine.

Each star is an echo of hopes on the rise,
The poetry of existence unfolds in our eyes.
Through infinity's arms, we shall wander and roam,
Finding refuge in verses that lead us back home.

Where Dreamspaces Converge

In realms where the dreaming and waking collide,
We meet in the spaces where mysteries bide.
With visions that shimmer, we weave through the night,
Where dreamspaces converge, painting futures so bright.

The fabric of time holds our thoughts in embrace,
In the hush of the twilight, we discover our place.
Through echoes and shadows, our spirits entwined,
We traverse the landscapes where hearts are aligned.

With whispers of starlight, we dance on the edge,
Creating a symphony, a vibrant pledge.
In the architecture of dreams, we build and explore,
Where love knows no limits, and souls can restore.

Together we wander through pathways unseen,
In the vastness of cosmos, we're forever the dream.
As stars gently witness our journeys converge,
In the heart of the night, our spirits emerge.

The Silence of Space.

In the stillness of the night,
Stars twinkle with pure light.
Galaxies drift, cold and deep,
Infinite secrets they keep.

Blackness wraps the vast expanse,
We spin in a cosmic dance.
Thoughts wander through the dark,
Each sparkle a celestial spark.

Time stands still amidst the void,
Where silence can't be destroyed.
Whispers carried on a breeze,
Echo through the timeless seas.

Yet within this void so grand,
Life dreams in starlit strands.
For where there's silence, hearts yearn,
In the cosmos, souls can learn.

Echoes of Celestial Dreams

Fading echoes call my name,
Wrapped in starlight, soft as flame.
Visions birthed from distant spheres,
Remind us of forgotten years.

In the dance of cosmic beams,
Life unfolds in vibrant schemes.
Stardust trails mark the way,
Guiding souls who chose to stray.

Galaxies hum a lullaby,
Underneath the velvet sky.
Each note spins a tale of old,
Of secrets that the stars have told.

Dreams of silver, dreams of gold,
In the vastness, time unfolds.
And as we gaze upon the night,
We glimpse the world beyond our sight.

Whispers from the Cosmic Abyss

Shadows swirl in endless space,
Whispers echo, soft embrace.
From the depths of void and time,
Mysteries in silence rhyme.

Fragments of a distant past,
In the void, our hopes are cast.
As comets sail through the night,
They carry dreams in their flight.

Stars align in silent pact,
Drawing hearts with gravity's act.
Each pulse a story to unfold,
In the dark, both brave and bold.

Here in twilight, shadows blend,
Journey starts, and journeys end.
Whispers linger, softly speak,
Of the stars we long to seek.

Dance of the Infinite Night

Underneath the midnight veil,
Galaxies swirl, stars set sail.
In the dark, they twirl and spin,
In an age-old dance, they begin.

Nebulas bloom like flowers bright,
Colors vibrant, pure delight.
Across the canvas of the sky,
The universe breathes, a cosmic sigh.

Planets spin in wild embrace,
In the rhythm of endless space.
As the cosmos paints its lore,
Each heartbeat a celestial score.

Embrace the night, let spirits soar,
In this dance, forevermore.
For in the silence, dreams ignite,
In the dance of the infinite night.

Celestial Dreams

In the night sky, stars align,
Whispers of hope, soft and divine.
A galaxy spins, stories unfold,
Dreams take flight, brave and bold.

Soft moons glow in silver hue,
Guiding the hearts that seek the true.
Endless paths in the cosmic sea,
Every heartbeat sets us free.

Waves of stardust kiss the dawn,
In the silence, we're reborn.
Floating high on wishes' wings,
Embracing all that starlight brings.

Beyond the veil where shadows play,
We chase the night, we greet the day.
Celestial dreams, a timeless chase,
Lost in wonder, found in grace.

Cosmic Whispers

Beneath the sprawl of darkened skies,
Cosmic whispers, the universe sighs.
Each twinkling light, a soft embrace,
In the silence, we find our place.

Nebula blooms with colors bright,
Tales of the cosmos, stars ignite.
Hidden worlds in the vast unknown,
Echoes of love in the great alone.

The night unveils its ancient lore,
Every pulse opens a cosmic door.
A dance of shadows and brilliant light,
In subtle breezes, they take flight.

In the warmth of dusk, truths collide,
We listen closely, with hearts wide.
Cosmic whispers, a lullaby sweet,
In their embrace, our dreams repeat.

Echoes of the Infinite

In the silence of endless night,
Echoes linger, pure and bright.
Voices of stars, a timeless sound,
In their rhythm, our souls are bound.

Galaxies swirl like a breathing sigh,
Infinite tales that weave and tie.
Moments caught in the vast expanse,
Lost in the magic, we twirl and dance.

Light years stretch, yet draw so near,
Whispers of fate we long to hear.
In the tapestry of time we weave,
Echoes of truth, we shall believe.

Distant stars in shimmering glow,
The path of dreams, forever flow.
In this journey, we find our way,
Echoes of love will never stray.

Lightyears Away

Across the void, lightyears away,
Time stands still, as moments sway.
Nebulas whisper through celestial streams,
Filling our hearts with tangled dreams.

Constellations map our secret paths,
In their glow, the darkness laughs.
Every star a lingering wish,
In the cosmos, we find our bliss.

A comet trails with fiery grace,
Chasing echoes through time and space.
In twilight's embrace, we hold our breath,
Searching the sky for timeless depths.

Distances fade, hearts intertwine,
In the silence, we find the divine.
Lightyears away, yet close in song,
In this universe, we all belong.

Across the Ether of Infinity

Stars weave in the cosmic silk,
Their light dances on time's brink,
Whispers of the universe glow,
In the void, our dreams flow.

Galaxies spin in silent grace,
A tapestry of endless space,
Through darkness, we seek the light,
In the ether, hearts take flight.

Celestial maps guide the way,
In the night, we boldly stray,
Mysteries wrapped in stardust dreams,
Reality is never as it seems.

Across the ether, we traverse,
In every verse, the cosmos converse,
Forever chasing fleeting sparks,
In the silence, we leave our marks.

Eclipsed by Celestial Whispers

In shadows cast by lunar glow,
Eclipsed secrets softly flow,
Celestial whispers drift through air,
Carried gently, tales laid bare.

Stars aligned in perfect grace,
Kindled glow on twilight's face,
Each flicker, a story told,
In moonlit nights, dreams unfold.

Galactic echoes, faint yet clear,
Calling forth what we hold dear,
Voices blend, creating song,
In the dark, we all belong.

Together we embrace the night,
In the depth, we find our light,
Eclipsed by whispers from afar,
We are woven, each a star.

Radiant Echoes of Lost Time

Fragments of a past now gone,
Whispers linger, like a dawn,
Through the cracks of memory's veil,
Radiant echoes tell our tale.

Moments dance in twilight's hue,
Fading gently, yet so true,
In the heart, they flare anew,
Chasing shadows as they grew.

Time slips softly through our hands,
Like grains of sand on distant lands,
Yet in the silence, we can find,
Radiant echoes, intertwined.

In every beat, in every sigh,
Our past sings sweetly, soaring high,
Though lost, it glimmers in the night,
In radiant echoes, we find light.

Echoes of the Fallen Comet

A comet streaks across the sky,
In its wake, the stars reply,
Echoes of a journey grand,
Whispers carried over land.

Fires blaze in luminous trails,
In the night, a tale prevails,
Each spark, a moment lost in flight,
Time unfolds in cosmic night.

Celestial wanderer, bold and free,
Leaving traces of history,
In the silence, watch it fade,
While dreams of wonder are laid.

Echoes linger, memories spun,
Connected threads, everyone,
In the cosmos, we find our way,
In the echoes, we forever stay.